The Transparency of Skin

The Transparency of Skin

Poems by Catherine Stearns

Minnesota Voices Project Number 36

NEW RIVERS PRESS 1988

Typesetting: Peregrine Publications
Front Cover Watercolor by Sally Langdon McCall
Back Cover Photograph of Ms. Stearns by Richard Klug

The author wishes to express her grateful acknowledgement to the following publications in which some of these poems, in slightly different form, first appeared. *Border Crossings, An Anthology of Minnesota Writers* ("The Hanging Horse," "The Bones of Small Animals," "Hair Which Can Be Magic Disappears"); *Calliope* ("Honeymooning at the Pamodzi"); *College English* ("Talking Back," "In the Park"); *Iowa Journal of Literary Studies* ("Playing in Bed"); *Iowa Woman* ("She Was a Gypsy"); *Modern Poetry Studies* ("Border People," "Blue Scarf," and "Summerhouse").

I wish to thank the McKnight Foundation in conjunction with the Loft in Minneapolis for a fellowship to help complete this book.

I would also like to thank the following individuals for their kind attention to *The Transparency of Skin* in manuscript: Allen Grossman, Sister Mary Virginia Micka, Clare Rossini, Vivian Vie Balfour and Bill Truesdale.

The Transparency of Skin has been published with the aid of grants from the Jerome Foundation, the First Bank System Foundation, the United Arts Council (with funds provided in part by the McKnight Foundation) and the National Endowment for the Arts (with funds appropriated by the Congress of the United States.)

New Rivers Press books are distributed by

The Talman Company   and   Bookslinger
150-5th Avenue   213 East 4th Street
New York, NY 10011   St. Paul, MN 55101

The Transparency of Skin has been manufactured in the United States of America for New Rivers Press, Inc. (C. W. Truesdale, editor/publisher) 1602 Selby Avenue, St. Paul, MN 55104 in a first edition of 1,200 copies.

This book is dedicated to Richard
with love and admiration.

When you know the house dark —
fraying carpet, turn, eleven stairs,
then you are home.

CONTENTS

III. Talking Back

I

The Unfinished Clock

*"Human events of the past may be fixed; but our
knowledge of them—which is history—is infinite."*
Raymond P. Stearns

". . . writing to pay what was not a personal debt."
Marianne Moore

Blackbird

At first it was just something in the road ahead of me,
                                          an obstacle
to my freedom
to catch a six a.m. plane and flee
briefly bound action and the given world.
Although I couldn't see clearly

I must have known it was a bird, one
of the hundreds of blackbirds or grackles or starlings
I've seen how many mornings, their iridescent
implosions, tease of meaning only
inches in front of me.

But this time meaning unfurled
and it had something to do with power.

Now I ask myself: Did I confuse mechanical habit
                      with passions to go on?
                      Did I forget—what I surely know—
                      that resistance sustains the flight?
                      Did I or did I not increase
                      the pressure of my foot upon the gas?

Simultaneously, a noise like the word *clock*,
                                    a pure absence of song,
and on my windshield an accordian of feathers, a shock
of blood. I saw
nothing behind me as I drove on.

3

Border People

*"We touch each other. With what? the beat of
wings."*

— *Rilke to Marina Tsvetayeva*

1.
The girl, balanced on one boot
on the bluish ice, knew the truth.
It was delicate and brutal, no more
than a whispered, preposterous word.

I have always imagined that if I could stop
her knowing, I could change everything:
the women who kissed her after the funeral,
the way she hated them because she thought
they would go home, put on white gowns
like wedding gowns, and watch the dark
waiting to be saved.
            The black and white
eiders moving into the wind
turned back that day, surrendering.

When her mother pressed her lips against the window,
tracing with her nails on the frost,
the girl saw and understood
that words were an elaborate code
done in reverse, decipherable
only from the inside.

2.
At a party, in elaborate disguise,
a woman, drunk, and with my mother's eyes
told me her theory of life:
We're all border people, she said,
living between worlds.

3. The Saltimbanques

(Picasso had begun an earlier painting underneath his
"Family of Saltimbanques")

Pablo, the angel, the shoulder man,
    lays her small hand
on a basket filled with roses—although
    it's not the season
for a garden. The others ignore the child.
    Sunlight strikes through
the canvas, lighting the cheap winter hats
    of fate and the woman
fingering her bare throat. Watch her
    breathe refusal
to the harlequin who wants to know.

    Oh, the child knows
and keeps her eyes down, wanting not to be
    beautiful, not to be
deferred by garments of green metallic silk.
    Is the woman the mother,
or who the child will become as she stares
    at the ground, still
soft on top and springy like a trampoline?
    For it is there—in her
mind's muscular leap at truth, beyond
    the windings of their legs—
that she sees the early shadows of desire,
    creatures like herself
wanting to pluck us from the other side.

4.
To get to my wedding,
I ran from the car and fell
on wet pine needles,
catching my hand on a wire fence
between the chapel and field.
Someone folded my hand in his
as if it had been severed, I remember
it beating like a wing alive.
And it was auspicious:
the hand didn't bleed.

Inside the church
everyone was waiting—
like the girl—
for the long march out of the dark hall.

Before I Married Anyone

Before I married anyone, I had a dream of your body
which by simple reason of its maleness
has always seemed to me so exposed, delicate
and unguarded. In my dream you were
naked and on your way to war.

Your eyes twinkled, I knew you wanted to go.
But I was afraid, and here's
where the dream needs confessing:
I wasn't afraid for you, no.
I was afraid you would survive
the battlefields, increase
your power.
                    I saw our fathers
before we were born, gazing
across the rooftops of an abandoned German town,
I saw them gather the stars about them,
I saw the stars streaming down,
and then I saw the stars
vanish within them.

Railroad Palace Queen

for my mother's mother's mother

Out West you cooked for the gandy-dancers,
men in gangs going up and down
on jiggers. You wanted to go to sea,
but your mother wouldn't hear of it.
From your grade-school reader, heavily underlined:

  You'll be a man my son.

But you'd be a gandy-dancer, our first
singer, sleepwalker, questioner.

                    *

Your mother had all those lovely sons
with crates of eggs under their arms
and you, with short red hair.
Later, a ghost in your bed.

Did she die in childbirth? They said
your father was screaming *she's dead, dead
get the undertaker*, so you
the oldest at twelve, dressed her
and combed out her hair.

And when you closed her eyes with pennies,
they said she twitched and pointed.

Somebody told the stories, which
of the old women was it
in black stockings and apron over apron?
You wrote "things" they said:
codes for a half-sleep
or images for waking in the dark?

Did you imagine your children
coming finally by twos by threes,
in groups like railroad cars:
Alma/Bella/Catherine, a corral of daughters,
little lizard girls like you
who could grow back a tail
after any injury?

*

Your words didn't survive you,
and the Railroad Palace photograph
does not speak. Nevertheless,
I heard voices fill with suspicious
delight whenever they said your name,

Susan Isabel McRaven:

Woman with a heart-shaped face, thin lips, eyes
unreadable, holding out
in familiar hands a fake one dollar bill.

My Grandmother's Saltbox

Dollhouse, circa 1900

The hinges, painted flat black, are for looks
only. The door stays shut. The handle's

paper-covered wire while bead-
covered wire makes excellent exotic

flowers, as if she'd found the familiar
American Beauties quite impossible.

For shutters she cut balsa wood with a pen-
knife — I remember the scar ringing

her finger — and with money saved
from her sewing bought the star,

a little magnet, above the door.
The pond reflecting her birds-of-paradise

is really a mirror — so I would imagine
myself at the center of this universe?

Inside the house, the strange and enormous
heads of dressmaker pins open the drawers

in which she kept everything that was hers:
earth / air / fire / salt-water

She Was A Gypsy

The bus is a bandstand drifting north.
After all my twenty-odd years
she is finally leaving my father. Now
mother and I, the only women on the bus,
sit at the back with the "Glo-Tones,"
bluesmen with mohair suits and diamond rings.
They talk of a jazzman on Basin Street who's disappeared.
My mother isn't listening, she sleeps
with a tight-lipped smile. To me
she looks guileless, worn out.
At the front of the bus an older man
who reminds me of my father
smokes his tenth cigarette since Scranton.
Small, short-legged, he might have been a jockey
before going to fat. When he shivers from an open window
I can almost see the horse-flesh knotted underneath.
I want to talk to my mother in a new way,
but she wakes up and talks about the weather.
When we come to the Howard Johnson's
she stares through the glass at the flurries,
her face outlined in the window
like a child's drawing. She drinks her coffee silently.
In the booth next to us a man reads
stock market quotes out loud. I say,
only to my mother, "first snow."

Is it all over in the bandstand
when age begins to pucker the dancer's thigh,
narrow her lips to an auctioneer's scowl?
First snow. When I was a kid
my mother's favorite poem was "Old Meg,
She Was A Gypsy." But she
never slept on the wild heath.
Hers is the talent for order,
for separating and sorting things.
I pay for her coffee, and we walk across the thin
snow in the glare of the Greyhound's headlights.

The motor hums, the door is open.
The traffic winds by in the slush.
Up and down the aisles I hear whiskey caps
unscrew. Outside the bus, the snow falls slowly,
sheer momentum and no mass.
One patch of clear sky: Venus
ploughs a furrow through it to the east.
Yes, Venus and I are all that's left
of the old gang, my family.
In my head I hear a new music, notes
that pinprick in the steelyblue
then slide off, rocking into space.
Later I try to sleep, but I see her round face,
fine almond eyes, black-lined and deep,
staring out the window. Everyone's healer.
Faces don't really age, I think;
beneath the sag, the hard set mouth,
they always lift, brutal and young.
Not like bodies that thicken or go slack
giving birth.

In the light green morning the bluesmen
fold like concertinas. We stop
at the border for a customs check:
Nothing, I repeat, to declare.
Farther north I hear the music of all-year snow,
but here it's slick cover, dried in spots.
A mile down the street the forests begin,
but everything else is ending.
The bluesmen collect in shuffling companies
at the glacier's hard rim. The old man waves.

My mother looks up. It's eight a.m.
and in the sky I see the afterimage of a moon.
The snow settles slowly on a northern brink.
"You know," she says to me, "I've never seen
Niagara Falls."

Imagined Daughter

Would she be a monkey on my back
or a thread leading me out

of this passionate gymnasium?
Would I polish her like an apple

for my father's desk or carry her
concealed in my mother's arms,

feeling only the brain-pulling hurt
of hair where she holds on?

Would she be an octopus, grabbing me
to her soft parts, using me up,

or a pilot fish tugging me
into the charmed circle of sun?

Would I make her flesh-thick with my milk,
or would she curl and close

like forced forsythia
that barely unfolds in water?

Would she run ownerless throughout the world
or make my hands a cradle, my feet take root

wherever, at last, I am?

Actual Son

He brings me the lavender heads of chive
I'd left to seed, not a gift exactly
but a token of his wonder: a flower!
in this mess of garden!

                         I'd imagined a girl.
But even before they jabbed the needle
into my tuffet of belly, I think I knew,
and felt my feminist womb betrayed.
Then my own wonder began: inside
me like a voice difference grew.
Once, feeling the thrust of his kick,
I thought (with not a little relish)
I have a penis! And I invoked Freud's mother
to share the joke. Without compunction

my son eats both flowers and weeds
and pulls up the marking sticks between.
Hybrids tap at the boundaries. I mean to tell him
that out of all the abundance of nature
these purple heads of chive are what I want.

Like Water

At times I think we've known everything
since the day we were born,
the clocks of our bodies knowing
just when the fist should open,
the knees propel us forward,
the mouth taste its own hard words.
We know so much more than we know
we know. Therefore,

when I remember the last conversation
I had with my father, who seemed
to be talking about the weather, trees
undone by wind, I know
how much of the ordinary tenderness
I've frittered away, time
like water through my hands, and

when I see my son finally sleeping
after hours of testing the world,
his will and his belly stuck out
as far as he can make them go,
when I see the way he seems to
breathe through his skin like a starfish,
I resolve to look and listen,
look and listen
to how much we know.

Twice-Born

I used to watch him through the keyhole
of his study door—cold, massive
desolate door, locked
from eight in the morning
until my mother came home at noon.
I couldn't see all of him but knew
he sat there in his green leather
chair with the sheepskin rug
over him, lost
in a book,
or with the hard flat board
balancing on his knees,
his own words like child-scratchings
on the yellow tablet before him.

Once, he called me in.
The tablet, like a neglected toy,
lay face-down in the corner.
He wanted me on his lap
to bounce up and down, up and down
until I was sick with the pleasure
and begged him to stop. But he wouldn't
stop   he
            opened
his knees and let me fall
through the creased trousers
into the dark into the fall
of all my later dreaming:
body jerking awake, mind outraged
until just before I fell too far
past the sudden power
of love, my father
grabbed me by the wrists
and pulled me in
to the world.

The Unfinished Clock

*"The best historians can do is to establish partial
truths and labor constantly to improve upon them."*
Raymond P. Stearns, historian
1904-1970

In the dark I hear the locusts
break open their husks
as the clock's endless ropes
pass over the pulleys.
Again I am a barefoot girl
in a white nightgown
on the cold boards of a house I left years ago
waiting for the clock to strike.

   The night before I left
you woke up and in the slur of dream-voice
called out my name, your mother's name:
the word *Catherine* divided

   "But the dividing lines are no more perceptible
   in the course of history than the lines
   of longitude and latitude are evident
   in the course of travel anywhere on earth."

Slowly, I learn how much space you occupy
in any place I live in, any page
no ink flows into, any time
no breath fills.
   When I try to pull you out
of history, you drag me in.

     *

In my dreams of you I'm stumbling
down known paths through blackberry canes
and happen on things that insist, that scratch,
drag their small hooks, draw blood.
Your hands, that could efface the world,
could still manage things gone wrong—
stopped clocks, hair with the devil in it—
could still set me right.

You talk to me until I come back
to the house. Time, you say,
to come home. I stop, look
at your outstretched hand:
a watery landscape, stories, my own
palm, lines
leading to where I am.

*

Once we sat together at Boothbay Harbor,
and a child walked out of the story you told
about *your* father, after his crops
had sunk into the same belly as the mud.
You found him killing a snake with a pitchfork,
again and again that rising and falling motion,
until he turned, finally, on you.
At the water's edge you stared down:
low tide and not the anticipated surge
but a thick green slag of seaweed,
as if the waves backing off too fast
had left only animal debris. You urged
the sea to move, MOVE, but for the moment
you are both still.

*

In your stories, such a gathering
of history without forgiveness. But if

    ". . . the shape and language of history
    are vitally affected by the historian,"

I re-write the balance
of salt against salt,

one drop and the Atlantic.
Your house is far away, moving fast
on its fabulous voyage,
but I keep your clock. It's time now
to begin:

                  *

I strip the old varnish off
to feel the hard wood underneath.
Most of the finish is gone, only traces
remain in the scarred pores of the grain.
Only time, like a rope to hoist us
past partial disclosures, unfinished
love, the turn and return of hands.

    Look, you said, inside
    the snail shell: you can see
    all the mutations of a line.

I rub steel wool deep
into the clock until the varnish
bubbles into tiny eruptions.
The stripper burns under my skin —
    my hands are split.

Singing in Bed

Desperate, he'd had the nurses

hang fishing line from the ceiling
to secure his music stand.
Once a womanizing trumpeter, now
an old man singing alone in bed.

He learned to turn the pages
with his tongue. He learned
to give the strings of his arms
to someone else's delicate touch.

The last time I heard him,
his A and my A sharp—
incapable of merging—
created a familiar sound:

no longer a god-father's sonorities,
nor yet the confetti of a harp,
just a song made

to break the silence.

II

Quickening

*"Conscience is like the heart, you can't just carve off
a little piece and walk on down the road."*
Bessie Head

Insomnia

Perhaps you can ruin your eyes by reading,
your reputation by talking, and
if you keep pulling on your lower lip
look like a gargoyle forever. Perhaps

your hands are never clean enough,
your body never good enough, and
your history of prolonged enchantment
will lose you hair, teeth, and money.

No doubt it's all on your Permanent Record.

So if love were offered like an orange crush
you would die, like you will anyway,
because if you can't say something nice
don't open your mouth because
if you don't open your mouth how
they gonna see that pretty girl smile because
if you don't lay your ghosts gladly
will they lay you.

Africa: First Night

No word but *jacaranda* between us. *Jacaranda*
turning blue and then bluer: imagine
blue dusk, blue dark.

In a dark night I hungered for sleep,
fanning myself with the words you believed,
words I could barely see, as unknown

as the children you taught whose bellies
puckered like old balloons, whose belief
I thought needed bread.

That first night we waited for each other
to speak. There was no moon, only
dark wings beating against dark walls.

When you said *jacaranda* to remind me
of the flowers we'd seen littering the dirt
of Kafue, turning blue and then bluer

until the ground was the sea, the sky—
slowly the dark became a blue dark, full
of your word again and, at last,

the leap into sleep.

Honeymooning at the Pamodzi

(The Pamodzi is an elegant hotel in Lusaka, the capital of Zambia. The speaker is a member of the Tonga tribe in Kafue, not far from Lusaka. Muka Joni means John's wife.)

I keep one eye open
to see what my husband does—
in his silk pajamas
he looks like a stranger.
This bed's big enough
for me and all my sisters
who are not yet married.
I am *Muka Joni, Muka Joni.*
Last night, I admit
I was a little girl
when he asked me to brush
my body with powder.
For the smell of dust
provokes the ghosts in my head.
Not that I won't adorn myself!
On my wedding day I tied
rattles and bells on my legs
when we danced in the daylight
where everyone could see
the tattoos on my chest
like palm fruit, the tattoos
on my back like stars.

This morning I missed
the roosters crowing,
my sisters shaking their gourds.
But I am *Muka Joni, Muka Joni.*
When I turn on a game show,
women like me
win pots and copper plates.
I think: I can be on TV
now I'm a rich man's wife.

25

Because I know
how to use the red ochre,
my bride-price was ten cattle.

At the Pamodzi there is water,
cold water and hot water,
but the roof is flat and low.
The roof of my mother's house
was laced with elephant grass.
I remember when death came
to fetch my little brother,
without even brushing the dust
off his buttocks, my mother
tried to hold him higher
than death could reach.
But when he comes—
in spite of rhinocerous horn,
crucifixes, dancing—
no one can resist.

My husband's lips are dry,
but not as cracked as earth
in the dry season.
He doesn't wake as I kiss him.
Downstairs, breakfast is
coffee and eggs and meat.
I won't have the meat myself,
though I think my husband will.
In the elevators are mirrors
to see how lucky I am—
Muka Joni. Muka Joni.
When I go to the swimming pool
surrounded by the high wall,
I swim up and down, hard

past the sirens in the street
and the girls I know out there
begging, and past their children
who move like poisoned fish.
When I finish,
I call for the towel-giver
(he looks like my cousin, Chamuka)
who forgets himself and hisses
at me, like a wounded snake.
How I laugh
in his unlucky face
when my new husband,
worth ten of him,
dresses upstairs in the military
and wears darkglasses
to shield his eyes
from the flies.

The Hanging Horse

—off a pier on the St. Lawrence River

whose two ears were delicate and as unlikely
to twitch as pointed ferns etched

on glass, whose coat gleamed
with the colorless fluid of some ghostly

libation, whose decorous head
smelled of a fear I recognized,

even as a child. Up near the tip of an iron arm,
rigid in the sling of two webbed bands,

his tail blown out straight in the wind,
the horse became a giant weather vane

and mine. For I cared then for something other
than myself, the heat of my love rising

and dipping with each frantic hoof
beneath his slick shoulders, and I knew

when I heard his moans that strands of fog
would loop out across the river forever.

The End of Childhood Comes Suddenly

1. *The Cormorants*

One abandoned August
a wild wind
came blowing.
Simple knots
at first, then
the hard cordknots
of muscle. Later,
although the leaves
curled and closed,
the earth cried
and the sea
snaked back on itself,
                              we saw
hundreds of sea-birds
nose-dive into the deep of it,
opening their wings like mouths

2. *Bloodsisters*

From Illinois we pitched suddenly forward,
two would-be women in faded jeans
crossing the land, skinny-dipping
in the Great Salt Lake,
eating the same pomegranate, ritual
of abiding sisterhood, and fighting
over each red seed. Fighting
because any difference threatened "betrayal".
Once, in a leaky tent in the Canyon de Chelly,
we lay so far apart that the water crept in,
soaking the limbs of our bodies
beautiful sea-green.

I was the one who threw the first stone.
It was winter, the stone
was ice, the wound
close to your eye.
In the cheap gilt frame of a motel mirror, I saw
  my blood on your face.

3. *The Sea*

I have saved almost everything I love

but your dream of the women flying
over a simple transparent sea.

Hair Which Can Be Magic Disappears

On the same day the eldest Ashanti daughter
has her head shaved —
an act of mourning
her chief and father —

another woman in a different country
is grabbed by the hair
from behind. Her first
bruises, like the royal-

blue cerements in Ghana, map
yet another country
from which the will
has been banished.

*

I used to let my hair fly like a child's
passion, although I was afraid
that one day I'd be riding
my red horse

and catch it, like Absalom, on a tree.
Then I learned to like the scissors'
shock of repeated sound,
and how I felt

stronger and lighter as hair fell down my back.
Sometimes I saw my father
hiding behind my mother's
dark hair-tent

that skirred over their wrists as they danced.
And when she cut it, I saw
the long line of her jaw
not unlike my own.

*

Once, at the Illinois State Fair,
I saw a woman tattooed with words:
when she flung the hair
away from herself

poems, connected by the body, appeared.

I Begin to Feel My Skin

(A woman testified that at twelve, when she learned her mother had died at Auschwitz, she buried her dolls in the back yard. Later, she dreamed she too had been buried under piles of dead bodies.)

Perhaps because I believed

in nothing, they thought me dead.
But I was not dead. I saw

the one in batiste and lace,
the glass eye in the bisque head,

the nostril with its diamond stud.
I savored the still-

fragrant orange blossoms
wired to the bride's small wrist.

When God said: *these were your children!*
Your own body's tenderness! I remembered

the weight of them in my arms,
the touch of their hair on my cheek.

But only when I'd thrown off their flesh
and inched my way to the eye

of light above me, did I begin
to feel my skin. Only

when I told him *do as you wish* was I
there, alive on the other side.

Blue Scarf

for S.

1.

You open your skin to get at your life.
You do this as if it's nothing
unusual. You open

your skin and presto!
a magician's scarf, long
and elegant, a silken
chain of lavender and deep blues.
You hold it up to the light, examining
each tiny hole. You tear
at the knots and seams
as if every day something small or stupid
must pay for its lack of excellence.

Remember, though, I've seen you.
Year after year, another face
in the mirror, seen you
send forth your doves
to no-one who loves you, seen you
carve with your knives
down to the barest bone.

2.

Some late afternoon when we are both old
I will tell you what I've seen. Over
the scarred china cups we will talk
not in the magic language we had as children
but as women alone with ourselves.
You will rub your fingers over your wrist,
as you always do, and throw the blue scarf
so carelessly around your shoulders.

The Bones of Small Animals

At times her life seems to have nothing
to do with her. She peels the vegetables,
fills the day with clutter of dishes, strangers,
perhaps a lover. She finds ways to speak,
finish dinner, go to bed. But she is not there,
not yet.

                She is remembering
the tall yellow house where she stood once
in the window, watching the men dig up
the garden. Nothing was supposed to be there,
nothing but the bones of small animals,
what she thought of as *things with no insides*.
Still, she expected something, someone
crouching in the dark hole.

First Marriage

after Pasternak

In the half-dark she once considered
Just how real she was,
Pausing to admire
A shaft of light showing there
The rare lines of her veins,
The shadows of her throat.
And then prepared the tenor of a deathbed scene.

Like precious jars
Brought by a god-father from Malay,
Lacquer in a dark cabinet,
She was too civilized to go into day.
She'd lost the broad patterns of wildness,
Lost the stoop of swallows over water.
She was all taut lines.

The lasting rain from the high plateau,
The lasting snow from the same place,
The deep circles,
                    ice and water,
Darkness, another spiral,
                              light.
She had not made strength from these things.

Hers was the virtue
Of the circle of fixed stars.
Who could have known
Who she was?

Trash

Epithalamium

Behind the church a great ditch runs
through a field of stylized trash

distance makes possible.
Here I am again, believing

if we bow low enough, like courting
birds, tin cans, banana peels

and motor oil will seem heroic.
Never mind commerce.

Here you are, irresistibly
promising the thing itself

while nature goes on trashing
our genius for advertising

with accidental assemblies
of half-torn labels in a ditch.

Never mind, darling. From here
they glint like diamonds in the sun.

I. Dread, or Domestic Life

Pregnant, naked, beached
in an armchair, I see

my hand tattooed with fleur-de-lis,
my ankles stiffen into wood.

Having been absorbed in a cloud of hair,
having known the transparency of skin,

having wanted and not wanted
my waters under a red star to break.

II. Childbirth

All winter I waited
preparing for the storm,
for the waves rising white
on the knuckles of the great Atlantic,
for the wind-strewn camellias
turning it instantly red.
In spite of my mother's silence
I thought I knew enough—
the shallows, the plunge,
the final irresistible explosion.
But at the real straits I roared.
Marvelling faces of sailors loomed up
until another cry,

                carried by the wind
out of unnamed waters,
echoed against my thin-skinned shore.

III. Expressing Milk

When I wake, my breasts have turned to stone.

My child sleeps through, so I slip
downstairs and lean over the basin, dipping
my hand into warm water, pouring it
over the granite contours. Pressing
in and out with thumb and forefinger,
I wait for the stone to bleed.

In unspeculating darkness, I wait
for the white ink of my body,
the perfect correspondence between need
and desire: mine and not mine.

Upstairs, my son uncurls
in steady, abundant dream.

Conversation With The-Poem-Not-Yet-Born

Alone in the room,
among books and silence.
It's dark and cold outside.
I peer at your outline
like a bedouin at a mirage,
like a diver at the ocean bed.
Will I find you
in the sand and shells,
break the ropes of seaweed
that hold tight your feet . . . ?

I started with you in a dark cellar
and unnumbered doorways. How slowly
we have entered, how unforgiving.

Oh, there are those who cracked their skulls
to be faithful to you, and you
were born and reborn endlessly.
I never stopped calling you,
although I was afraid. Asleep,
I strained my ears for your footsteps.

I have found you in a hand I held,
a fist unclenching, in the V
at the trench of the neck. Always
in the glass-black blood within.
In the laundromat, in the street.
I have dragged you out
of history. Tonight
how will you come to me?

III

Talking Back

"It is necessary to remember and to choose."
Louise Bogan

"The aim of attachment is detachment."
from *A Manual of Childcare*

Talking Back

Outside the locked church
of my childhood, there was an alley
and a wizard who spread out

his most obedient fingers
one by one and one by one
four quarters appeared, all for me
if I promised — swore —
never to say anything to anybody.
Now,

　　　freedom is not a sudden thing,
and a kid afraid of the infinite
longings doesn't say much anyway.
But I learned to look at people:

Do the feet show vanity or trouble?
Do the hands show wealth or trouble?
Do the eyes show sorrow or trouble?

And when I was older I looked
at the way the women curled
their shoulders to hide their breasts,
and the way the men looked
at the women.

　　　Without words
it took a long time to believe
in the likeness of us. Finally,
inside the flesh of my body I stood
up and began to talk.

In Response to a Male Friend's Query

No, not much like a sneeze, unless
        you're driving faster
than the rain down Highway 101 north
        of San Francisco to Eureka
and nonetheless the sun is shining on the whole
        left side of your body

        including your bare toes
and on the radio Joan Sutherland's high
        high E-flat from *Lucia*'s
Mad Scene pierces the almost inaudible
        rasping of dust particles
bouncing off metal, cloth, skin, when
        suddenly the need's so great

        that your leap from the planet
is no longer conscious: you skid gloriously,
        clumsily into the shoulder
and drive again and again right past yourself.

The Last Run

They cut the last run through northern Minnesota
a month ago, and yesterday a talkative miner, a woman
with a notebook, and a boy crazy or high enough to punch out

a rear window with his fist, rode the last knotted miles
of the East Kentucky leg to McGriff and Hale City.
If you could gather the dust that blows south from Tempe

and carves up the yellow wind to Deming, if you could ride
through the ancient rhythms and really listen
in the Carolina wetlands as copperheads pop under the tires,

if you could catch the line before it leaves, you
could catch "what it is that's dying in this country"
and hold it like that boy, trembling in nobody's arms.

Grief Is The Work Of The Heart

—for R., whose mother died when he was young

Go now
from the bedroom to the door
recalling, precisely, the hand's contour
as she closed the door behind her.
Rapunzel's hair undulated
like the rapids of a dangerous stream
you read before anyone knew.

Go now
from the door to the window
where outside her flowery curtains
a robin comes close
enough—almost—to touch,
its belly brighter than the beak
of the statuary duck
leading her family through the garden.

Go now
from the window to the table
where an inconsolably lonely man
left a rabbit's foot and a ring
from his King Edward's cigar.
The ring was gold, remember,
and the delicate webs of tobacco
internal membranes, a tattoo
of veins, leading finally to the heart.

Go now
from the table to the heart.

Tom Canetti

Holding my son, I make myself
imagine his soft body, vulnerable
in its nakedness, fat little knees and elbows,
Buddha-belly, the papery skin of his genitals

—I make myself imagine this boy too
confronting the terrors of war.
That this perfect body settling into sleep
could one day understand "strength"
as a gathering of perfect bodies
dead . . .

I make myself remember Vietnam and Tom
Canetti, who happened to be male,
facing the absolute cold with a lottery number,
and I try to feel
his fear   smell the burning
but the unthinkable lies here with my only son

Water Color

(for my friend's daughter, born blind)

In darkness, we would end
by being blind. But to begin
in darkness . . . ?

        Holding you hungry
against her breast, she used to wonder
could you see in to yourself? The cells
of your eyes alive on the other side
looking deep into the head, straight
into the heart? If thought
is inward language, what strange sights
might you have?

Not less real, I know now
as I watch you paint a reddish dot
that swims like a perfect fish
and grows, vertically,
through layers of horizontal color,
each vein a distinctly clearer blue.
What does it look like, you ask,
knowing it is not a fish at all
but "The Magic Eye" to be
taped to the refrigerator door.

          *

Once, through a hospital window I saw
a gold sphere of goat's-beard contract to a dot.
From the first, little pilot fish,
your magic eye saw what mine did not.

You Can Only Give What You Have

—from a country western song heard on the radio
on the way to my grandfather's funeral

At night I dreamed my dreams
floated vaguely through the streets,
resting at the far hills' feet then
asleep forever at the foundry door.

Now, my grown son thinks, *It's my turn*
and all my children who were
my book and my harp and echo,
loosen my grip and fly away.
Someone called to me: *Rise,
Herman, rise and shine.*
Covered in sweat, the body shines.

When did I cease to be
the hawk my sons rode each evening
past the lonely hills, the tree
my young wife leaned up against?
Only the very old, men whose ribs
I could have snapped, knew
covered in sweat, the body shines.

Each day I'd remember my father
and my father's father
naked to the waist, pulling
their shovels from the fire.
When molten metal hit the air
sparks flew out like birds
and I cried *Ah! Ah!* with the rest.
Covered in sweat, the body shines,
the body shines.

Summerhouse

The mattress on the floor is stained with roses
darker than those outside the door
where, in spite of the heat, her daughter plays.
Every summer she hears her voice
trying to name a crazier garden:
Lamb's-quarter? Chicory? Annie's Lace.

All the familiar, unremembered things
top a bureau: habitat of guide books,
a doll made out of shells. In the dust
of a corner she writes her daughter's name.

Again she is a guest in an old and friendly place
where well-water is cold when she cups it,
where willows bow low to the ground,
and the dark grass of her mother's hair
grew wild as fireweed.

At the Monuments

Zennor, Cornwall

In front of an ancient monument, my son
squints, laughs self-consciously, and finally smiles
at his father who waits, camera in hand,
for his son to be himself. Behind them
the stones have shifted, evolved
like our bodies

*

If he reached back
            and down
my son could touch the cold deposit
of our humanity. And they are cold,
these monuments,
           so cold
I almost want him to withdraw
his hand, as I did when

I asked my father: do you believe in God?
Bear in mind, he said, the corresponding things within.

*

I move away, onto other ruins
but my son stands still and quite alone.
He studies the ancient face, its tragic detail,
seeing there I trust the seasoned
stone, healing sun, recognizing
something caught and held.

And So You Speak

for Marvella Spicer

Working like I do, my neighbor says, takes it all
out of you. You come home, eyelids flickering
neon, kick off your shoes, sit and stare
at the window. You want to be pleasant,
crack a joke or two, but there's this fist
in your mouth, the words don't start
crystal clear. You shrug just to make
your body move.

Clearly, you have to say something
clearly, but the old ponderous words
of your parents, the ones you even remember,
aren't any use, and the new ones
the new ones are as cold as
the T.V. or the back of your ex-
husband's hand.

When you finally look
right at what you love most in this world
you can't say exactly: is it a pale yellow light
or your child's bright hair?
You are tired, the noise makes no sense
until you remember what it is
you would die for, and so
you speak.

Reading

"Oh, tell us, poet, what do you do?"
— Rilke

In the midst of the general noise
of traffic and our desire
to be anywhere else, the poet
who has been dead for years
rolls away his tightly-woven bandages
and the fat of our hearts
to give us a story, perhaps
a revelation.

When it's over, we raise
our eyes to the bare walls,
the muzak and the cigarettes.
Not that we hate the daily
army of voices, but
there was a certainty
in suddenly seeing our names,
and now we seem to be losing
track. A door opens:
which side of it are we on?

Having held us in his gaze
for so long, the poet found
he did have something to give us.
Not the mysterious, consoling
tales we thought we wanted,
but something to go on with,
to tend and to keep. Simply
the fact, as we walk
down the stairs and out
into the street, as we begin
imagination and invent
the poet, simply the fact
of familiar eyes upon us.

In the Park

Sewn on the seas of lawn
are we all here?
Families gathering their blankets and baskets, quarreling a little;

young men in unnecessary leather jackets walking quickly by
with an air of purpose and enigma;
a boy called Mario suddenly leaping into the air;

a father holding three identical straw hats by their elastic bands,
pointing at the lake with an iron father look
as his giggling daughters stare at the five or six
couples closing their eyes between the trees, unaware
      that the incandescent blue pours directly over them;

two men stretched out on a chaise-lounge, one
too thin, the stretched skin of his face
contorted with pain, he looks beyond the air while his friend
      strokes his forehead, his arm;

a gang of kids following a punker pushing a red motorcycle
with a raccoon tail smoking at the heel of the rear mudguard.
He keeps looking back, so tenderly . . .

One old woman on a bench with her book and knees open
writing (I imagine) *forever, why not forever*
each mirroring the whole mystery of one another's
past and present and future

and each blind to the signals. Too soon
she gets up, finding her way among the lake and clouds,
slipping in free under the skyline.

CATHERINE STEARNS was born in Illinois in 1952. Her father, to whom "The Unfinished Clock" is dedicated, was a professor of history at the University of Illinois. Her mother, who once taught in Zambia, is a retired historian now living on Cape Cod. Ms. Stearns attended Beloit College and the Writers' Workshop at the University of Iowa, and in 1985 received her Ph.D. in English and American Literature from Brandeis University. She has received grants from the Iowa Arts Council and was a recipient in 1984 of the Loft-McKnight Award in Poetry. She has taught at the University of Iowa, Macalester College, and The College of St. Catherine. She recently moved with her husband and son to Wellesley, Massachusetts.